Some months before his death Sir Max Beerbohm gave his blessing to a project for the recovery and presentation in book form of some of the best and least available of his caricatures. He also approved the plan of a series of such volumes, each devoted to a decade of his work, and made known his preferences for the contents of this first volume, *Max's Nineties*, which covers the years 1892–1899.

Of the forty-six drawings included, only eleven have previously appeared in a book; nine of them in Max's first collection, *Caricatures of Twenty-Five Gentlemen*, which was published in a limited edition in 1896, one in the Penguin edition of *The Poets' Corner*, and one in Bohun Lynch's *Max Beerbohm in Perspective*. The others are all reproduced from the nineties periodicals in which they first appeared—*Pick-me-Up*, the *Idler*, *Vanity Fair*, the *Butterfly*, the *Academy*, the *Savoy* and so on, with the exception of a series of eleven drawings entitled 'Mr Gladstone goes to Heaven' (1898), which have never, so far as is known, been reproduced before.

The other subjects range from writers and artists (Whistler, George Meredith, Henry James, Aubrey Beardsley, George Moore) to politics (Joseph Chamberlain, Balfour, Labouchère), the theatre (Ada Reeve, Arthur Roberts, Wilson Barrett) and as far as the Duke of York (afterwards King George V) and Napoleon at St Helena.

1961

1961

MAX'S NINETIES

1. SELF-CARICATURE
circa 1893

MAX BEERBOHM

MAX'S NINETIES

Drawings 1892 - 1899

With an Introduction by Osbert Lancaster

RUPERT HART-DAVIS: 36 SOHO SQUARE W.1

1958

Publisher's Note

This book originated in the mind of the late Allan Wade. He had admired and collected the work of Max Beerbohm since the late Nineties, and he pointed out that a large number of the early drawings had never been collected from the periodicals in which they first appeared. A series of three or four volumes was planned, each devoted to a decade of Max's work, and Allan Wade produced copies of a large number of drawings made in the Nineties. A selection of these was sent to Sir Max. He approved the general scheme, but rejected some of the drawings as unworthy of resurrection. In their place he suggested nine drawings from his first collection, *Caricatures of Twenty-Five Gentlemen* (1896), and the set of eleven called "Mr Gladstone Goes to Heaven".

The only drawings which have been reproduced from originals are the frontispiece (by kind permission of Lady Beerbohm), "Oscar Wilde" (by kind permission of the Ashmolean Museum, Oxford), and "Mr Gladstone Goes to Heaven" (by kind permission of the Junior Carlton Club). The frontispiece has already been reprinted in *Max Beerbohm in Perspective* by Bohun Lynch (1921), but, so far as is known, Mr Gladstone's apotheosis is here reproduced for the first time.

Nos. 12–20 have been reproduced from *Caricatures of Twenty-Five Gentlemen*, and the others from the following periodicals: 2 is a selection from two issues of the *Strand Magazine*; 3 and 4 from the *Pall Mall Budget*; 6–10 from *Pick-me-Up*; 11 from the *Savoy*; 21 from *Vanity Fair*; 22 from the *Chap Book* (Chicago); 23 from the *Saturday Review*; 24–26 and 46 from the *Academy*; 27 from the *Sketch*; 28 and 29 from the *Daily Chronicle*; 30 and 34 from the *Idler*; and 31–33 from the *Butterfly*. 5 was reprinted in the King Penguin edition of *The Poets' Corner* (1943).

On being asked whether he would contribute a few notes about some of the subjects, Sir Max wrote, on 6 November 1955, "Here and there I might write a brief critical note about the drawing or the person. But of course the drawings must mostly speak for themselves." They have been allowed to do so, for before the notes were written Sir Max died on 20 May 1956 at the age of eighty-three.

PRINTED AND BOUND IN GREAT BRITAIN BY
THE BOWERING PRESS, PLYMOUTH AND THE
LEIGHTON-STRAKER BOOKBINDING CO. LTD
LONDON

Contents

Introduction

Max Beerbohm, despite the fact that happily he continued to flourish well into the second half of the twentieth century, has generally been regarded, and rightly, as essentially a figure of the Nineties. He was seventeen when the decade opened, and descending on London a year or two later, almost immediately became the Benjamin of a group that inspired a half-appalled fascination in the majority of their contemporaries, and retained for posterity so powerful a charm that they came in retrospect to embody a whole epoch, which, incidentally, was also adorned by such considerable, though notably less glamorous, figures as Rudyard Kipling, Thomas Hardy and Bernard Shaw. But although the youngest personage in the definitive conversation piece, 'Some Men of the Nineties', with which, some thirty years later, Max registered his surprise at the continued interest the period inspired, there never appears to have attached to him any of the immaturity of youth. "The gods," said Oscar Wilde, "have bestowed on Max the gift of eternal old age."

Insofar as his literary works alone may be taken as evidence, the theory that Max was spared all normal growing-pains and sprang, fully equipped, from the head of some more sophisticated Zeus, appears incontestable. And it could well be said of him, as he himself said of Beardsley, that he "achieved masterpieces at an age when normal genius has as yet done little of which it will not be heartily ashamed hereafter." But in the matter of his earliest drawings the case is slightly different. Although charming, frequently accomplished, and invaluable as documents for the study of the period, they are still some way from always displaying the certainty and assurance of his mature style. A great part of the interest which attaches to the present collection lies, therefore, in the opportunity it affords us of studying in the embryonic stage what were to become some of the artist's most noteworthy characteristics, of noting mannerisms which he was subsequently to abandon, and of reassuring ourselves that there was indeed a time when he, too, who was latterly to appear so alarmingly self-sufficient, so totally and invariably himself, was, like the common run of artists, subject to false starts and responsive to influences from without.

Of the two great traditions which had flourished in English comic art during the nineteenth century, one was at this date showing signs of exhaustion. Worked by the accomplished, the too accomplished, hand of du Maurier, the vein of domestic and social satire, so richly exploited by Leech and Keene, was producing but feeble rewards. From those charmingly drawn upper-class, after-dinner scenes every sign of visual humour had been rigorously purged, and the captions underneath, for all their relevance to the subject-matter of the picture, might as well have been advertisements for deaf-aids. Fortunately for *Punch*, the principal guardian of the sacred flame, there now emerged a brilliant draughtsman, Phil May, whose swift, economical line always carried that directly humorous emphasis which du Maurier had long since lost beneath an overlay of delicate shading and elaborate cross-hatching.

For Phil May Max always expressed the greatest admiration and affection, but, save perhaps for the single instance of his drawing of the artist himself (3), where the intention is clear, he made no effort to borrow from Phil May's style. Instinctively, maybe, he realised that his own approach to the problems of draughtsmanship was essentially conceptual, and that from an artist whose work had so firm a visual basis as Phil May's there was little that he could safely learn.

The school of single-figure, portrait caricatures that had originated with the elder Dighton at the end of the eighteenth century was, on the other hand, in the Nineties still robust and flourishing. The weekly *Vanity Fair*, to which Max himself soon became a contributor, had for more than thirty years been regularly publishing coloured caricatures of figures prominent in contemporary life, framed collections of which today render so many country-house billiard-rooms and club corridors valuable for students of Victorian personality. Of the various artists who contributed to the series the greatest, and the most consistent, was undoubtedly "Ape" (Carlo Pellegrini), for whom Max's admiration always remained unbounded. His successor "Spy" (Leslie

8

Ward), who was just at this time beginning to take over, had modelled his style so assiduously on that of his senior as to make their productions almost indistinguishable. Latterly the element of caricature in his work was steadily reduced, and many of the drawings Spy published during the first decade of the present century approximate almost to portrait miniatures. To this unfortunate deviation Max's practice was to provide a valuable corrective.

The influence of these men, patent and acknowledged, is, in the present volume, perhaps most clearly detectable in the drawing of George Meredith (21), but Max was far too original an artist to adopt any tradition, no matter how exalted, without substantially modifying it. He was also the friend and admirer of Aubrey Beardsley and a devotee of the Pre-Raphaelites (he confessed, in the course of a speech on the occasion of his seventieth birthday, that his earliest ambition had been to be a painter in the style of Burne-Jones), and the finest examples of his mature style may perhaps be said to represent the time-honoured tradition of Ape, to which the aesthetic lessons of the *Yellow Book* had been delicately applied by a literary genius with a strong vein of purely visual fantasy. Of the drawings in the present volume it is perhaps only that of Whistler (30) from which the reader will be likely to form an adequate idea of the shape of things to come.

Although, as one likes to think, a peculiarly English phenomenon, Max belonged to a group which enjoyed far closer contacts with the world across the channel than did the majority of English artists, and there were at least two great French contemporaries of whose work he was keenly and profitably aware. In the period covered by this book, Sem (of whom in the next decade Max was to publish an admirable likeness) was only at the beginning of his career, and it would be fanciful to look for traces of his influence, but Caran d'Ache was at the height of his powers, and the very first plate in this book, 'Club Types', affords evidence that his example was not without its effect. (Incidentally in these drawings, which were some of the very first of Max's to be published, it would be hard indeed even for the expert to detect the Master's hand. Only the figure representing Brooks's, or so it seems to me, could be reasonably sure of a correct, if hesitant, attribution.)

In assessing the value of these early drawings in relation to Max's work as a whole there is one final point to bear in mind. When he started his

9

career as a cartoonist the technique of mechanical block-making by photographic reproduction on zinc was in its infancy. For magazine work the artist was virtually confined to the line-block, or the even more hazardous half-tone of the period, and as a result Max was too often compelled to do with a pen, assisted by inefficiently applied mechanical tint (see for example the drawing of Squire Bancroft, 9), what he was far better equipped to achieve with pencil and brush. In this connection it is instructive to compare the effect of the splendid series of Gladstone drawings, here reproduced from the original drawings for the first time, with those taken from his first published collection *Caricatures of Twenty-Five Gentlemen* (1896), the originals of which have long since disappeared. For it is as true of him as it is of Rowlandson that as a technician he was primarily a great water-colourist, and until processes of reproduction were sufficiently advanced his work could be fully appreciated only by those fortunate enough to see it in exhibitions.

Now in the Junior Carlton Club.

There remains one further point; all his life Max's most fruitful inspirations derived from the backward glance. Of many of the figures in this book — George Moore, Arthur Balfour, Oscar Wilde — he was to continue to make drawings for almost half a century, and the most penetrating, the most deeply felt versions of these recurrent and familiar themes were achieved only when the subjects were at long last unblemished by any distracting suggestion of immediacy. Art for him finally resolved itself into once-disturbing figures recollected in tranquility. And whereas in the Nineties he may well have been tranquil — it is difficult to picture him as ever having been anything else — he had, as yet, very little profitably to recollect. In this present collection it is, therefore, those figures who had already acquired the status of myths — Gladstone, Harcourt, Whistler — of whom his presentation most clearly foreshadows the lines along which his gifts were, for more than four decades, so splendidly to develop.

OSBERT LANCASTER

ATHENÆUM

WHITE'S

REFORM

ST. JAMES'S

SAVILE

NATIONAL LIBERAL

GUARDS'

BROOKS'S

SAVAGE

2. CLUB TYPES

3. PHIL MAY

4. GEORGE GROSSMITH

5. OSCAR WILDE

6. ADA REEVE

7. JULIA NEILSON

8. EARL SPENCER

9. SQUIRE BANCROFT

max

10. PADEREWSKI

11. ARTHUR ROBERTS

12. HENRY LABOUCHERE

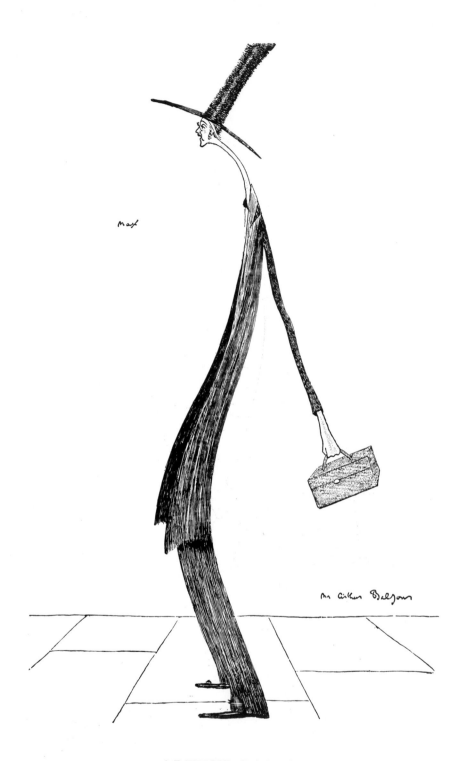

13. ARTHUR BALFOUR

14. SIR WILLIAM HARCOURT

15. AUBREY BEARDSLEY

16. HENRY HARLAND

17. SIR GEORGE LEWIS

JOSEPH CHAMBERLAIN

MAX

18. JOSEPH CHAMBERLAIN

19. GEORGE MOORE

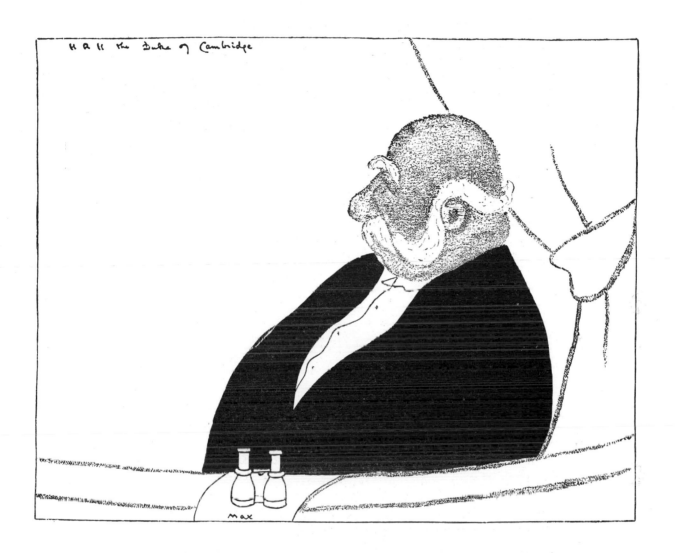

20. H.R.H. THE DUKE OF CAMBRIDGE

21. GEORGE MEREDITH

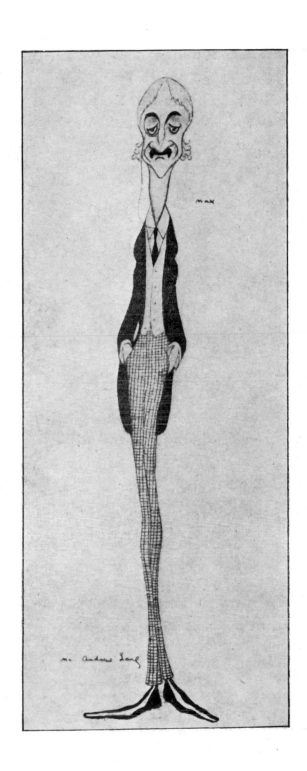

22. ANDREW LANG

23. WILSON BARRETT AS MARCUS SUPERBUS

24. A. B. WALKLEY

25. R. B. CUNNINGHAME GRAHAM

26. HENRY JAMES

27. ROBERT HICHENS

28. WILLIAM ARCHER

29. CELTADES AMBO:
EDWARD MARTYN and W. B. YEATS

30. A NOCTURNE:
MR WHISTLER CROSSING THE CHANNEL

31. H.R.H. THE DUKE OF YORK

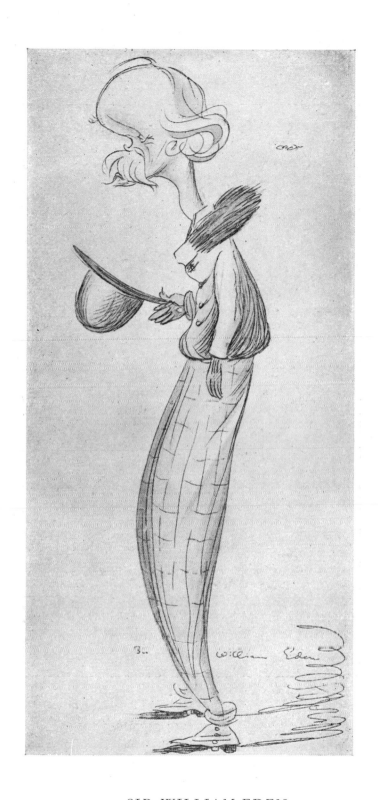

32. SIR WILLIAM EDEN

33. NAPOLEON AT ST HELENA

34. HALL CAINE

35 - 45. MR GLADSTONE GOES TO HEAVEN

Saves now in the Junior Carlton Club

I. St. Peter, having had his orders for some time, refuses admittance to Mr Gladstone. Mr Gladstone then commences to speak—"It was a great effort, worthy of a great occasion," wrote the Reporting Angel. "Never had the Old Man Eloquent spoken with more fire and force, nor employed his inexhaustible resources of dialectic to greater effect." The O.M.E. is here proving that Heaven was one of his birth-places. The simple ex-fisherman gradually falls under "the wizard spell of his eloquence" and, in order to avoid the peroration, unbars the gates of gold and pearl.

II. The same evening Mr Gladstone addresses a mass-meeting of Angels. He pays an eloquent and graceful tribute to God.

III. The Old Adam. On leaving the meeting, Mr Gladstone picks
up a fallen angel.

IV. Next morning, Mr Gladstone narrowly escapes an awkward
rencontre with General Gordon.

V. Cut by the Prince Consort!

VI. Homer recognises his footstep.

VII. He passes beneath Horace's window.
"*Ego* docebo te perdere mea carmina!"

VIII. He meets Mr Parnell.

"Oh, Mr Parnell, don't be so hasty! Give me two hours and a
half, and I can explain all to you!"

IX. The Last Straw.
Mr Gladstone reading the name of one of the principal streets.

X. His departure from Heaven.

"Certainly not! I presume you are paid your wages?"

XI. The End.
Peace with Sulphur
"And one clear call for me."

46. SELF-CARICATURE